Mushroom Grower's Diary

Genus/Species	Cultivation Method	Substrate Blend

Flush #	Source LC Agar _____ Other	Lighting Method	Temp Control

Dates	
Recieved	
Inoculated	
Colonization	
Spawn Shaken	
Begin Fruiting Conditions	
Pinning	
Cultivated	

Flush total Weight: Fresh _____   Dry _____

Notes

Week 1	M	T	W	T	F	S	S
Fan							
Mist							

Notes

Week 2	M	T	W	T	F	S	S
Fan							
Mist							

Notes

Week 3	M	T	W	T	F	S	S
Fan							
Mist							

Notes

Week 4	M	T	W	T	F	S	S
Fan							
Mist							

Notes

Week 5	M	T	W	T	F	S	S
Fan							
Mist							

Notes

Week 6	M	T	W	T	F	S	S
Fan							
Mist							

Notes

Genus/Species	Cultivation Method	Substrate Blend

Flush #	Source LC Agar _____ Other	Lighting Method	Temp Control

Dates

Recieved	
Inoculated	
Colonization	
Spawn Shaken	
Begin Fruiting Conditions	
Pinning	
Cultivated	

Flush total Weight: Fresh _____   Dry _____

Notes

Week 1	M	T	W	T	F	S	S
Fan							
Mist							

Notes

Week 2	M	T	W	T	F	S	S
Fan							
Mist							

Notes

Week 3	M	T	W	T	F	S	S
Fan							
Mist							

Notes

Week 4	M	T	W	T	F	S	S
Fan							
Mist							

Notes

Week 5	M	T	W	T	F	S	S
Fan							
Mist							

Notes

Week 6	M	T	W	T	F	S	S
Fan							
Mist							

Notes

Genus/Species	Cultivation Method	Substrate Blend

Flush #	Source LC Agar _____ Other	Lighting Method	Temp Control

Dates	
Recieved	
Inoculated	
Colonization	
Spawn Shaken	
Begin Fruiting Conditions	
Pinning	
Cultivated	

Flush total Weight: Fresh _____   Dry _____

Notes

Week 1	M	T	W	T	F	S	S
Fan							
Mist							

Notes

Week 2	M	T	W	T	F	S	S
Fan							
Mist							

Notes

Week 3	M	T	W	T	F	S	S
Fan							
Mist							

Notes

Week 4	M	T	W	T	F	S	S
Fan							
Mist							

Notes

Week 5	M	T	W	T	F	S	S
Fan							
Mist							

Notes

Week 6	M	T	W	T	F	S	S
Fan							
Mist							

Notes

Genus/Species	Cultivation Method	Substrate Blend

Flush #	Source LC Agar _____ Other	Lighting Method	Temp Control

Dates	
Recieved	
Inoculated	
Colonization	
Spawn Shaken	
Begin Fruiting Conditions	
Pinning	
Cultivated	

Flush total Weight: Fresh _____ Dry _____

Notes

Week 1	M	T	W	T	F	S	S
Fan							
Mist							

Notes

Week 2	M	T	W	T	F	S	S
Fan							
Mist							

Notes

Week 3	M	T	W	T	F	S	S
Fan							
Mist							

Notes

Week 4	M	T	W	T	F	S	S
Fan							
Mist							

Notes

Week 5	M	T	W	T	F	S	S
Fan							
Mist							

Notes

Week 6	M	T	W	T	F	S	S
Fan							
Mist							

Notes

Genus/Species	Cultivation Method	Substrate Blend

Flush #	Source LC Agar _____ Other	Lighting Method	Temp Control

Dates	
Recieved	
Inoculated	
Colonization	
Spawn Shaken	
Begin Fruiting Conditions	
Pinning	
Cultivated	

Flush total Weight: Fresh _____   Dry _____

Notes

Week 1	M	T	W	T	F	S	S
Fan							
Mist							

Notes

Week 2	M	T	W	T	F	S	S
Fan							
Mist							

Notes

Week 3	M	T	W	T	F	S	S
Fan							
Mist							

Notes

Week 4	M	T	W	T	F	S	S
Fan							
Mist							

Notes

Week 5	M	T	W	T	F	S	S
Fan							
Mist							

Notes

Week 6	M	T	W	T	F	S	S
Fan							
Mist							

Notes

Genus/Species	Cultivation Method	Substrate Blend

Flush #	Source LC Agar _____ Other	Lighting Method	Temp Control

Dates

Recieved	
Inoculated	
Colonization	
Spawn Shaken	
Begin Fruiting Conditions	
Pinning	
Cultivated	

Flush total Weight: Fresh _____   Dry _____

Notes

Week 1	M	T	W	T	F	S	S
Fan							
Mist							

Notes

Week 2	M	T	W	T	F	S	S
Fan							
Mist							

Notes

Week 3	M	T	W	T	F	S	S
Fan							
Mist							

Notes

Week 4	M	T	W	T	F	S	S
Fan							
Mist							

Notes

Week 5	M	T	W	T	F	S	S
Fan							
Mist							

Notes

Week 6	M	T	W	T	F	S	S
Fan							
Mist							

Notes

Genus/Species	Cultivation Method	Substrate Blend

Flush #	Source	Lighting Method	Temp Control
	LC Agar ——————— Other		

Dates

Recieved	
Inoculated	
Colonization	
Spawn Shaken	
Begin Fruiting Conditions	
Pinning	
Cultivated	

Flush total Weight: Fresh _____   Dry _____

Notes

Week 1	M	T	W	T	F	S	S
Fan							
Mist							

Notes

Week 2	M	T	W	T	F	S	S
Fan							
Mist							

Notes

Week 3	M	T	W	T	F	S	S
Fan							
Mist							

Notes

Week 4	M	T	W	T	F	S	S
Fan							
Mist							

Notes

Week 5	M	T	W	T	F	S	S
Fan							
Mist							

Notes

Week 6	M	T	W	T	F	S	S
Fan							
Mist							

Notes

Genus/Species	Cultivation Method	Substrate Blend

Flush #	Source	Lighting Method	Temp Control
	LC Agar _____ Other		

Dates	
Recieved	
Inoculated	
Colonization	
Spawn Shaken	
Begin Fruiting Conditions	
Pinning	
Cultivated	

Flush total Weight: Fresh _____   Dry _____

Notes

Week 1	M	T	W	T	F	S	S
Fan							
Mist							

Notes

Week 2	M	T	W	T	F	S	S
Fan							
Mist							

Notes

Week 3	M	T	W	T	F	S	S
Fan							
Mist							

Notes

Week 4	M	T	W	T	F	S	S
Fan							
Mist							

Notes

Week 5	M	T	W	T	F	S	S
Fan							
Mist							

Notes

Week 6	M	T	W	T	F	S	S
Fan							
Mist							

Notes

Genus/Species	Cultivation Method	Substrate Blend

Flush #	Source LC Agar _____ Other	Lighting Method	Temp Control

Dates	
Recieved	
Inoculated	
Colonization	
Spawn Shaken	
Begin Fruiting Conditions	
Pinning	
Cultivated	

Flush total Weight: Fresh _____   Dry _____

Notes

Week 1	M	T	W	T	F	S	S
Fan							
Mist							

Notes

Week 2	M	T	W	T	F	S	S
Fan							
Mist							

Notes

Week 3	M	T	W	T	F	S	S
Fan							
Mist							

Notes

Week 4	M	T	W	T	F	S	S
Fan							
Mist							

Notes

Week 5	M	T	W	T	F	S	S
Fan							
Mist							

Notes

Week 6	M	T	W	T	F	S	S
Fan							
Mist							

Notes

Genus/Species	Cultivation Method	Substrate Blend

Flush #	Source LC Agar —————— Other	Lighting Method	Temp Control

Dates

Recieved	
Inoculated	
Colonization	
Spawn Shaken	
Begin Fruiting Conditions	
Pinning	
Cultivated	

Flush total Weight: Fresh _____   Dry _____

Notes

Week 1	M	T	W	T	F	S	S
Fan							
Mist							

Notes

Week 2	M	T	W	T	F	S	S
Fan							
Mist							

Notes

Week 3	M	T	W	T	F	S	S
Fan							
Mist							

Notes

Week 4	M	T	W	T	F	S	S
Fan							
Mist							

Notes

Week 5	M	T	W	T	F	S	S
Fan							
Mist							

Notes

Week 6	M	T	W	T	F	S	S
Fan							
Mist							

Notes

Genus/Species	Cultivation Method	Substrate Blend

Flush #	Source LC　　　Agar _____ Other	Lighting Method	Temp Control

Dates

Recieved	
Inoculated	
Colonization	
Spawn Shaken	
Begin Fruiting Conditions	
Pinning	
Cultivated	

Flush total Weight:　Fresh _____　Dry _____

Notes

Week 1	M	T	W	T	F	S	S
Fan							
Mist							

Notes

Week 2	M	T	W	T	F	S	S
Fan							
Mist							

Notes

Week 3	M	T	W	T	F	S	S
Fan							
Mist							

Notes

Week 4	M	T	W	T	F	S	S
Fan							
Mist							

Notes

Week 5	M	T	W	T	F	S	S
Fan							
Mist							

Notes

Week 6	M	T	W	T	F	S	S
Fan							
Mist							

Notes

Genus/Species	Cultivation Method	Substrate Blend

Flush #	Source LC Agar _____ Other	Lighting Method	Temp Control

Dates	
Recieved	
Inoculated	
Colonization	
Spawn Shaken	
Begin Fruiting Conditions	
Pinning	
Cultivated	

Flush total Weight: Fresh _____   Dry _____

Notes

Week 1	M	T	W	T	F	S	S
Fan							
Mist							

Notes

Week 2	M	T	W	T	F	S	S
Fan							
Mist							

Notes

Week 3	M	T	W	T	F	S	S
Fan							
Mist							

Notes

Week 4	M	T	W	T	F	S	S
Fan							
Mist							

Notes

Week 5	M	T	W	T	F	S	S
Fan							
Mist							

Week 6	M	T	W	T	F	S	S
Fan							
Mist							

Notes

Genus/Species	Cultivation Method	Substrate Blend

Flush #	Source LC Agar _____ Other	Lighting Method	Temp Control

Dates

Recieved	
Inoculated	
Colonization	
Spawn Shaken	
Begin Fruiting Conditions	
Pinning	
Cultivated	

Flush total Weight: Fresh _____   Dry _____

Notes

Week 1	M	T	W	T	F	S	S
Fan							
Mist							

Notes

Week 2	M	T	W	T	F	S	S
Fan							
Mist							

Notes

Week 3	M	T	W	T	F	S	S
Fan							
Mist							

Notes

Week 4	M	T	W	T	F	S	S
Fan							
Mist							

Notes

Week 5	M	T	W	T	F	S	S
Fan							
Mist							

Notes

Week 6	M	T	W	T	F	S	S
Fan							
Mist							

Notes

Genus/Species	Cultivation Method	Substrate Blend

Flush #	Source LC Agar _____ Other	Lighting Method	Temp Control

Dates	
Recieved	
Inoculated	
Colonization	
Spawn Shaken	
Begin Fruiting Conditions	
Pinning	
Cultivated	

Flush total Weight: Fresh _____   Dry _____

Notes

Week 1	M	T	W	T	F	S	S
Fan							
Mist							

Notes

| | | | | | | | |

Week 2	M	T	W	T	F	S	S
Fan							
Mist							

Notes

Week 3	M	T	W	T	F	S	S
Fan							
Mist							

Notes

Week 4	M	T	W	T	F	S	S
Fan							
Mist							

Notes

Week 5	M	T	W	T	F	S	S
Fan							
Mist							

Notes

Week 6	M	T	W	T	F	S	S
Fan							
Mist							

Notes

Genus/Species	Cultivation Method	Substrate Blend

Flush #	Source LC Agar _____ Other	Lighting Method	Temp Control

Dates	
Recieved	
Inoculated	
Colonization	
Spawn Shaken	
Begin Fruiting Conditions	
Pinning	
Cultivated	

Flush total Weight: Fresh _____   Dry _____

Notes

Week 1	M	T	W	T	F	S	S
Fan							
Mist							

Notes

Week 2	M	T	W	T	F	S	S
Fan							
Mist							

Notes

Week 3	M	T	W	T	F	S	S
Fan							
Mist							

Notes

Week 4	M	T	W	T	F	S	S
Fan							
Mist							

Notes

Week 5	M	T	W	T	F	S	S
Fan							
Mist							

Notes

Week 6	M	T	W	T	F	S	S
Fan							
Mist							

Notes

Genus/Species	Cultivation Method	Substrate Blend

Flush #	Source LC Agar _____ Other	Lighting Method	Temp Control

Dates	
Recieved	
Inoculated	
Colonization	
Spawn Shaken	
Begin Fruiting Conditions	
Pinning	
Cultivated	

Flush total Weight: **Fresh** _____   **Dry** _____

Notes

Week 1	M	T	W	T	F	S	S
Fan							
Mist							

Notes

Week 2	M	T	W	T	F	S	S
Fan							
Mist							

Notes

Week 3	M	T	W	T	F	S	S
Fan							
Mist							

Notes

Week 4	M	T	W	T	F	S	S
Fan							
Mist							

Notes

Week 5	M	T	W	T	F	S	S
Fan							
Mist							

Notes

Week 6	M	T	W	T	F	S	S
Fan							
Mist							

Notes

Genus/Species	Cultivation Method	Substrate Blend

Flush #	Source LC Agar —————— Other	Lighting Method	Temp Control

Dates

Recieved	
Inoculated	
Colonization	
Spawn Shaken	
Begin Fruiting Conditions	
Pinning	
Cultivated	

Flush total Weight: **Fresh** _____   **Dry** _____

Notes

Week 1	M	T	W	T	F	S	S
Fan							
Mist							

Notes

Week 2	M	T	W	T	F	S	S
Fan							
Mist							

Notes

Week 3	M	T	W	T	F	S	S
Fan							
Mist							

Notes

Week 4	M	T	W	T	F	S	S
Fan							
Mist							

Notes

Week 5	M	T	W	T	F	S	S
Fan							
Mist							

Week 6	M	T	W	T	F	S	S
Fan							
Mist							

Genus/Species	Cultivation Method	Substrate Blend

Flush #	Source	Lighting Method	Temp Control
	LC Agar _____ Other		

Dates	
Recieved	
Inoculated	
Colonization	
Spawn Shaken	
Begin Fruiting Conditions	
Pinning	
Cultivated	

Flush total Weight: Fresh _____   Dry _____

Notes

Week 1	M	T	W	T	F	S	S
Fan							
Mist							

Notes

Week 2	M	T	W	T	F	S	S
Fan							
Mist							

Notes

Week 3	M	T	W	T	F	S	S
Fan							
Mist							

Notes

Week 4	M	T	W	T	F	S	S
Fan							
Mist							

Notes

Week 5	M	T	W	T	F	S	S
Fan							
Mist							

Notes

Week 6	M	T	W	T	F	S	S
Fan							
Mist							

Notes

Genus/Species	Cultivation Method	Substrate Blend

Flush #	Source LC Agar _____ Other	Lighting Method	Temp Control

Dates

Recieved	
Inoculated	
Colonization	
Spawn Shaken	
Begin Fruiting Conditions	
Pinning	
Cultivated	

Flush total Weight: Fresh _____   Dry _____

Notes

Week 1	M	T	W	T	F	S	S
Fan							
Mist							

Notes

Week 2	M	T	W	T	F	S	S
Fan							
Mist							

Notes

Week 3	M	T	W	T	F	S	S
Fan							
Mist							

Notes

Week 4	M	T	W	T	F	S	S
Fan							
Mist							

Notes

Week 5	M	T	W	T	F	S	S
Fan							
Mist							

Notes

Week 6	M	T	W	T	F	S	S
Fan							
Mist							

Notes

Genus/Species	Cultivation Method	Substrate Blend

Flush #	Source LC Agar _____ Other	Lighting Method	Temp Control

Dates

Recieved	
Inoculated	
Colonization	
Spawn Shaken	
Begin Fruiting Conditions	
Pinning	
Cultivated	

Flush total Weight: **Fresh** _____   **Dry** _____

Notes

Week 1	M	T	W	T	F	S	S
Fan							
Mist							

Notes

Week 2	M	T	W	T	F	S	S
Fan							
Mist							

Notes

Week 3	M	T	W	T	F	S	S
Fan							
Mist							

Notes

Week 4	M	T	W	T	F	S	S
Fan							
Mist							

Notes

Week 5	M	T	W	T	F	S	S
Fan							
Mist							

Notes

Week 6	M	T	W	T	F	S	S
Fan							
Mist							

Notes

Notes & Observations

Time to reorder for the next flush! If you enjoyed this book please let me know what was most useful in your review!

Don't forget to check out the other books in this series:

Foraging & Spore Print Logbook
Magical Microdosing Calendar Diary
Trippy Trip Tracker - Heroic Dose Reflections

Coming soon:
Mushrooms are Magical - A Psychedelic Coloring Book for Stoners & Psychonauts

Made in United States
North Haven, CT
03 March 2023

33508902R00054